THE

THE WILL TO BE FREE

A Philosophy for Young People

Valentin Wember

TEMPLE LODGE
London

Translated by Eva Knausenberger

Temple Lodge Publishing
51 Queen Caroline Street
London W6 9QL

Published by Temple Lodge 1999

Originally published in German under the title *Vom Willen zur Freiheit, Eine Philosophie der Jugend* by Verlag am Goetheanum, Dornach, Switzerland, in 1991

A catalogue record for this book is available from the British Library

ISBN 902636 08 2

Cover by Studio MAOSS
Typeset by DP Photosetting, Aylesbury, Bucks
Printed and bound in Great Britain by Cromwell Press Limited, Trowbridge, Wiltshire

Contents

Foreword

This book by Valentin Wember, whose central topic is the will to be free, is the result of the author's working relationship in word and deed with young people. Burning life issues, such as the will to be free, confront young people especially between the ages of 15–20, when life is faced with its conflicting situations and a myriad of inner and outer problems which arise through interactions with friends of the same age or older. Only rarely though do young people wish to plough their way through thick books of philosophy in order to solve their problems.

But a small, easily read booklet such as this one may provide a helpful and stimulating support, for it systematically examines by using practical life situations the existential question of the will and the ways to be free.

Every chapter, every page lends itself to further contemplation or discussion.

The direction and focus of human striving tends to become obscured in the course of varying relationships, discussions, tasks and conflicts. If, however, this booklet is carefully studied, either alone or together with friends, it can become a helpful preparation for times of inner strife and an aid towards forging the next steps in one's own development. It is my hope that this booklet may find many energetic, focused and goal-oriented young readers.

Jörgen Smit,
Goetheanum, February 1991

Preface

Dear reader

Now that you have opened this book you are probably hoping to gain something from reading it. This, however, will only happen under certain conditions which need to be outlined so that you do not start with false expectations and risk disappointment. The first condition is that you have a lively interest in the issue, namely, the human desire to be free. The topic is worthy of serious thought and warrants more than mere theoretical curiosity. The issue itself is life-sustaining, life-enhancing and is more than a gymnastic exercise for the mind. You must also not be put off by the fact that the word 'freedom' is much used and much abused in our modern society, and that the label often has little or nothing to do with the reality of the matter.

As you can see from the title, we are dealing here with the human *will to be free*. We are not trying to *prove* that we are free but to find out in what sense we can become free when we really want to be. The second aspect of the title indicates that we can become free if we *activate* our will forces, and it is indeed a particular kind of will that we are going to look at in the course of the book.

You may well wonder why the subtitle is: 'A philosophy for young people'. As a rule philosophies are not written for young people, rather the contrary is true. For instance, Aristotle, the Greek philosopher, excluded young people from his discourses because he said their age stood in the way of understanding. Rudolf Steiner, however, suggested in the early 1920s that a philosophy ought to be written especially for young people. Together with his co-worker Maria Röschl, he intended to rewrite his book *Die Philosophie der Freiheit* (the English title is sometimes translated as: *The Philosophy of Spiritual Activity)** for young people. The booklet in your hands is an attempt to produce what he had in mind. It has its foundation in anthroposophy, a fact that needs to be remembered. This booklet is a first attempt at rewriting *Die Philosophie der Freiheit* for young readers, a few chapters of it at least. The work will be continued in a further publication.

---

* Editions currently in print are *The Philosophy of Freedom* (London: Rudolf Steiner Press 1999) and *Intuitive Thinking as a Spiritual Path* (New York: Anthroposophic Press 1995).

1. The Question

Deep within every human being dwells the yearning to be free. Yet it seems as though the impulse to be free is constantly under siege, is hemmed in, put to sleep or drowned out. But is it ever dead? Can it be killed? Experience shows that the longing to be free can lie dormant for decades until one day it suddenly springs to life. Like a last spark buried underneath an ash heap, it may suddenly and unexpectedly burst into all-consuming flames. Does this always happen? Do we know of cases where the spark stays buried? Might that be true for most of us? Are there perhaps mountains of ash which not only bury but totally smother it? Is it not true that increasingly the load of rubbish dumped on us is heavy enough to render the notion of being free a mere illusion and empty talk?

Questions like these need thorough testing. If this is lacking we will be left with opinions based on a mixture of half-digested insights, theories and feelings. In forming opinions we mostly start out with such half-digested insights, theories and feelings which are also very fluctuating. But an *opinion* is not true *knowledge*, not genuine insight. Thus our goal should be to advance from mere opinions to genuine knowledge lest they have disastrous consequences for our actions. If, for instance, our belief proves to be wrong that inner freedom today is both possible and attainable, we shall base our actions on false premises and render them meaningless. The goal we have in mind would then not be within our reach but swept aside by reality or irretrievably buried. If, on the contrary, our opinion is that the aim to be free is simply an illusion whereas in truth this is not so, then our resulting actions would also lack meaning and be filled with an air of resignation where such resignation is unnecessary. We need therefore to shoulder the task of taking a close look at all these questions to attain real understanding beyond the web of half-baked opinions. Only then will the consequences we wish to draw for our actions rest on solid ground.

2. Imprisonment

Let us begin by looking at some situations in which we do not feel free. Demands and restrictions are one example. They definitely give us the feeling that we are not at liberty to do what we want to do. They are, for the most part, imposed from outside. In childhood they come from parents, in youth from teachers, in adult life from the boss and legal authorities such as the state. Parents can forbid our doing something we want to do—maybe not directly, but they can impose conditions which prevent our original plan. We often feel limited and constrained. Similarly teachers or instructors, superiors and professors at the university intervene by imposing restrictions that hamper us in the extreme, until we no longer feel free to do what we intended to do. The same holds true for the government which imposes a myriad of regulations that direct and limit us: the speed limit, tax laws and social regulations, military ordinances we may or may not agree with. All these limitations have one thing in common. They are imposed from outside. They hamper us so that we feel unfree. A second common feature is that they are imposed by an authority. Whoever makes regulations and ensures they are obeyed possesses authority and power. It need not go beyond a certain scope, but we are dealing with the power of authority as long as obedience can be enforced. In a true life situation it means, for example, that if someone stands in the way of my wish to travel it inevitably forces me to wonder: 'How do I cope with the authority holding me back? Several options are open: I can rebel against both and yet submit to them. Reasons for such a decision can vary. Maybe there is little to be gained by rebellion except a whole lot more trouble. Maybe there is neither the inclination nor the will to fight. Perhaps I can accept the prohibition on the grounds that, all things considered, it is not as unfavourable as I first thought. Indeed I may be able to use it to my advantage. Another alternative is to do it my way, come what may.'

Every person has a different way of dealing with factors that encroach on one's ability to choose freely, because each of us is endowed with different character traits. In other words, no two people react in exactly the same way. This difference can be so marked that what appears as a constraint to one, even an insult to self-determination, may not trouble another person in the least. How we react depends greatly upon the mental attitude of the individual. If we carry this thought with us for a while we can make a small but significant discovery.

As stated before, limiting decrees are imposed from outside. Their effect, however, is primarily determined by the recipient, by one's own attitude towards them. Insight into this fact may reduce my negative reaction. True, the prohibition may hit me with full force and I may feel a score of emotions. But since I am not an automaton, my thinking capacity will lead me to ask: 'Might other people react quite differently? Do I have a choice of reaction?' As soon as such thoughts come to life within me the process of free will development has begun. I gradually assume the power to make my own decisions when I no longer leave that task to others. The extent to which I feel unfree depends on me. Also, while I am thinking, the emotional impact diminishes perceptibly. Not that it disappears altogether, but it does become more manageable. This then is the gift of the small insight that says: 'Everything that comes to me from outside sources can determine me only to a limited degree. Most of it is up to me.'

Let us now explore if the same holds true for other limitations imposed from outside, such as those from friends, parents, teachers, bosses and the government. Some children suffer greatly from the family into which they were born. The mere fact that they have to live together with their parents and siblings gives them the feeling of being in a spiritual dungeon. Acquaintances and friends are part of life's circumstances. Though there are varying degrees of intimacy, truly happy relationships are rare. More often than not we chafe under the yoke of having to live and work together with certain people in schools or work-places, feeling that we cannot live or unfold the way we really want to. There are a multitude of reasons. At times we feel like outsiders, lonely and unaccepted by the group, without really knowing why. We may suffer from the shallowness or deceit of others, their laziness, arrogance or intellectual superiority, which render us silent and withdrawn, until we enter into a state of internal emigration by trying to ignore the troublemakers. Though such reactions are chosen as a likely way out, others are possible. We may openly rebel or try to change the behaviour of others, or we may, as a last resort, leave altogether. But as a rule the latter choices are made only after a lot of suffering and after other means have failed.

Friendships are important to almost everyone. But friendship, harmony and closeness often end when possessiveness, domineering instincts and fear creep in, when friendships become the contrary of what we had actually hoped for. At times power struggles of demonic proportions seem to imprison us. They may last for months, even years, and while they last they seem to rob us more and more of the very air we need to breathe and to be free. Most astonishing, however, is the duration of such conflicts, their cruel refinement and intelligent finesse. Later on we can only wonder why we submitted to such psycho-terror for so long a time. What is it that seems to paralyse us beyond reason? We may think that such treatment and behaviour in our friendships is due to powers that originate in other people, but if we think about it for some time we will find out that much is due to our own internal configuration. We do not always remember that friendships are not in themselves a guarantee of happiness and harmony and that a failed friendship may not be entirely blamed on others. We have to face the fact that often we are too lazy and not creative enough to make the friendship work. Why is that?

Creativity demands a willingness to change a given form, which means above all that we must be willing to change ourselves. To develop creativity is not easy and many people unconsciously shun the effort. Instead they yearn for the finished product, a friendship rich in happiness and harmony. A more motivated individual might say the following: 'Why should I want something that is already done? I want to have a creative influence on my relationships. As long as I wait for the friendship I have in mind, I am dependent on forces beyond my control. If I wait passively for something to come my way, I have to take what comes. If harmony comes my way, very well, but in that case I am happy only as long as it lasts and afterwards I am still dependent on external events. But if I do not wish to be a slave of the situation, if I want to have an input, I will have to exert a formative influence on it.'

There is something fascinating about such a strong line of thought and yet we may not feel altogether at ease with it. The philosopher J.G. Fichte was a man who desired above all to be independent of people's ever-changing moods and ideas about happiness and unhappiness. He wished to owe his success to his own creative striving. He went so far as to maintain that it really should not matter whom we marry, because we all ought to have enough strength of character to change, and that loving our spouse is only a matter of will. If Fichte is right we could add the thought that the wish to see our chosen partner change is solely due to the fact that we ourselves lack the necessary strength of character to evolve. And further, that our desire to be loved suggests that we are not able to actively love other people and would rather wait passively for love to come to us.

No doubt, such powerful thoughts are fascinating and sound convincing to those who have experienced the joys of creative decisions and spiritual will impulses. Yet Fichte's idea, which is founded on the conviction that human beings need not be dependent upon anything but their own creativity, also has something harsh and repellent about it. It sounds one-sided because Fichte does not mention, nor does he seem to notice, that relationships are 'more' than the sum total of our will impulses, however active and creative they may be. Hölderlin summed up this 'more' in the words: 'Ere we ever met, we were meant for one another.' The profound feeling of belonging together, of being meant for each other, stems from another realm than our present constitution.

It is thus also not necessarily right to blame a failed friendship on a lack of creative willing or active love. Relationships are not merely blocks of stone which, through creative effort, can be transformed into a sculpted work of art, as Schiller once put it. A relationship has a life of its own; it cannot be arbitrarily fashioned. For this reason some friendships are doomed from the start. And though the failure may leave us with a feeling of despair and restriction, we may have to admit that impulses and reasons integral to our personality and part of our internal make-up led to the demise of the friendship.

If these thoughts are borne out by experience, they prove that the feelings of not being free, as far as bonds with friends, family members and authorities are concerned, are only partially imposed upon us from outside. The other part is due to our own personal inner constellation.

Let us follow this train of thought, because it is a key element in finding out how we can become free. Geographical, cultural and historical realities are further factors to be reckoned with in our life-environment. It is of consequence whether we were born in France or Germany, Tanzania or Alaska. A good number of research projects have studied the effects of the mother tongue on people's thoughts and perceptions.

The language researcher Helmut Gipper for instance reported that the Navaho Indian language has only one word for both green and blue. The attempt was made to find out whether these Indians really lack the ability to distinguish between the two colours, whether their visual nerves and brain structure prevent such a distinction. The results showed that although the Indians found it difficult to distinguish between green and blue the problem was not so much a function of their optic nerves but of their language, which had never challenged them to see the difference. Scientific studies of this nature suggest that our origin within a given language influences our seeing and thinking habits. People who speak several languages will confirm that they prefer one language over another when it comes to expressing certain concepts. Does this not also mean that our mother tongue limits our means of free expression, since it compels us to perceive and think in a certain fashion? We can of course learn more languages, but won't the benefits always be very small?

A further possible limitation is geographic location. In other words, it matters where we live. One person may have to live in the city with its noises, fumes and congestion and find city life most constricting. He rails against the fact that he cannot find a quiet living environment, while another one may 'die' of loneliness in the freedom of the countryside. The impediment of the environment is blamed; forests, meadows, streets and high-rise apartments are reviled, as if it were their fault that we are not free.

What we see here is a collision of objective realities on the one side and our own wishes and ideals on the other, where both together bring forth a sense of being hopelessly entangled.

Finally, of great significance is the time in which we live. Not everyone is happy to be born in the twentieth century. Our modern times carry with them a sense of continual stress, their orientation is overwhelmingly materialistic and, above all, we have hanging over our heads like the sword of Damocles all manner of possible man-made catastrophes.

All of the above affect us in some way. More than anything else, however, the twentieth century has a changed attitude towards the question of inner human freedom by comparison with earlier centuries. The introduction of nuclear energy, for one, will force many future generations to deal with the problem of atomic waste. No one in the foreseeable future will be able to say: 'We are no longer interested in the scientific accomplishments of our forefathers because we are going to change all that.' Though future generations may quite possibly find a solution for the safe disposal of atomic waste, such discoveries have yet to be made and so we, and those after us, will have no free choice in the matter. We are forced to deal with it. We are also not free to ignore many of the other technical legacies of the twentieth century.

Certainly, in the past great inventions have been made as well, such as one that had a very far-reaching influence, namely, the printing press. Yet it is conceivable, in theory at least, that the world would go on if no one ever read another printed book, and the consequences were accepted. But there is no way around nuclear technology. (This argument is no plea for increased nuclear development. It rather refers to the insidious nature of nuclear waste that is in part now lying in corroding drums on the ocean floor.) Modern technology has enslaved us more thoroughly than we have ever been before. It is truly so, though there are those who would argue to the contrary. We can remember Goethe's ballad *The Sorcerer's Apprentice*. In the story the apprentice manages to engage some supernatural powers for his own purposes, only to find that he is unable to control and direct them. In the end he has to acknowledge that '...the spirits I called forth I cannot get rid of again'. In Goethe's ballad the master himself finally comes back to put an end to the nightmare. He sends the spirits back to their rightful place. One wonders who the master is today or will be in the coming centuries?

The man-made enslavement then that emanates from modern civilization is the most massive form of enslavement possible. We feel its paralysing effects everywhere and few people, with some notable exceptions, feel able to fight against it in a meaningful way. Has anything changed since the disaster at Chernobyl? Does war really improve relationships between industrialized nations and the Third World? Will the production and export of weapons be reduced in the foreseeable future?

In the face of such questions our thoughts run through various alternatives and yet, in the end, we cannot but conclude that they come to a halt at the end of blind alleys. Erich Fromm (a German educator) pointed out that consumers have a lot of power and he called for consumer boycotts. Products not purchased would become redundant. If, for instance, cars were no longer bought this would have to lead to a new perspective in life. But seriously, how could anyone hope for a change, given the multiplicity of consumers and consumer interests. The trend of television and the press is: We amuse ourselves to death. (Also the title of a book by Neil Postman.)

The technological advances of mass production have brought about unprecedented individual powerlessness and lack of freedom which leave us with few alternatives. We therefore tend to ignore the issues and relegate them to areas aside from conscious contemplation. If, hour after hour, we thought and worried, we could hardly go on living in any meaningful way. (A Centre has been established in Holland where permanent care is given to people who have become psychologically ill from the effects of thinking about the destructive nature of our civilization.) Once we realize that we cannot simply ignore the problems that have come upon us through modern technology, we are also called to learn to cope with the resultant feelings of helplessness and defeat.

We have not, however, come to an end of the catalogue of external factors contributing to our feeling of not being free. Among them are sudden bereavements—the loss of a beloved person, illnesses, strokes of destiny. If we are suddenly called to care for a much loved but seriously ill person, we are faced with a task we would probably not have freely chosen. It is put upon us from outside and we have the choice of fulfilling the task with inner resistance or of earnestly but voluntarily making it ours. It is a matter of specific thoughts and feelings we develop towards this new life situation. The same holds true if we ourselves become ill or injured and our life is given a new and unforeseen direction. Whether we become miserable and depressed or whether we find reasons that help us deal emotionally with the outer forces of destiny, lies within our freedom of choice.

Outstanding examples of how to deal with a particularly difficult destiny have been given by the people involved in the resistance movement against Hitler and the Third Reich during the Second World War. One story is as follows. During the night of 23–24 April 1945 a group of men were taken across a bombed out and ruined section of Berlin. They were political prisoners from Moabit prison who had been told that they were to be relocated in preparation for their imminent release. Instead, they were shot and killed right there in the ruins. We owe this information to one of the prisoners, a young Communist, who had been shot in the head but survived by pretending to be dead. In the pockets of one of the executed prisoners there were later found some blood-spattered sheets of paper. In a tiny pencilled script were written a number of poems which, in the course of time, became known as the *Moabit Sonnets*. The author's name was Albrecht Haushofer. These poems document the resilience of the human spirit and the will to survive with integrity under appalling circumstances. They show that the light of inner freedom can be kindled in feelings and thoughts even in prison.

Haushofer's understanding, evolved during his incarceration, is this. The reason I am not free is not primarily due to the fact that I have been brutally imprisoned. I am in bondage because my soul is in the clutches of invisible, fettering principles which keep it from soaring freely. The bonds that enchain the soul are, according to Haushofer, automatic reflexes, passions, drives and other instinctive patterns of behaviour.

In one sonnet called *The Mosquito* he describes his encounter with a mosquito during the winter months in his cell in Moabit prison:

The Mosquito

The faintest humming sound. On to my hand
a tiny midget settles, wings awhirr,
a breathlike body, and six fragile limbs
whence did it come into this wintry land?
Its stinger readied ... should I squash it now?
do I begrudge the drop of blood that nourishes
the little beast? The itch, the pain inflicted?
It acts because it must. And will I do the same?
Go on then, bite, you little winged soul
as long as this, my blood, is nourishment
as long as it may see you through another day.
Bite then, so that you never lack in strength!
We are, midget and man, both little else
but shadows, coming from the One Great Light.

This remarkable encounter between mosquito and man awakens in Haushofer the realization that human beings can act freely. He could regard the instinctive and reflex-induced act of killing in order to avoid pain as an unfree act. In another sonnet he expresses gratitude for his imprisonment, because it became his means to go forward from inner bondage to inner freedom. It is likely that Haushofer was bound hand and foot for a long time and that, for a few weeks at least, the chains had been removed. The poem following is his answer to the question: 'What is the nature of freedom and what things really fetter human beings?'

Freed from Bondage

Some weeks now have I been from fetters free.
I hardly know how many moons it's been
if long if short the time they bound
and whether they will bind me once again.
And yet they taught me that some other chains
are not so ready to let go. Desires, cravings
which the child, the man, the grizzled beard
cling to, with stubborn eagerness,
are chains around the heart, turn hearts to stone.

The will-born lusts, that Buddha once spoke of
and Christian folk know as the hard'ning sin
are jailers that deny the healing grace.
If I am free, more free than e'er I've been
I owe it to my body's chained and shackled state.

The message of both poems is this. Even a physical state of
imprisonment does not, of necessity, have to be experienced
as a lack of freedom; it may indeed be the avenue leading to
inner freedom. Can we ourselves learn the same lesson?
Perhaps we will never be imprisoned, but severe illnesses are
a form of imprisonment as well. The loss of a beloved person
feels like a bereavement, an accident may rob us of our
freedom of movement. Such things happen and may become
the occasion for feelings of helplessness and duress. So let us
now take a look at the 'gaolers' within our souls.

3. Setting Ourselves Free

While imprisoned, Albrecht Haushofer came to realize that inner-human constellations contribute much more to the feeling of bondage than actual imprisonment. He further realized that the key to inner freedom is ours when we rid ourselves of our internal 'gaolers'. These powers that have a hold on us are called: instincts, drives, desires and passions. Almost all of us have experienced that our emotions can run away with us. If something runs away with us, almost against our will or better judgement, we have before our inner eye the picture of a horse running away with the rider. The rider is supposed to rein in the horse, the horse should follow the rider's command.

The picture below is of an ancient Greek statue of a charioteer. He is clearly quite in command of both horses and chariot. If you look closely you will no doubt realize that the

stance of the charioteer is not conducive to guiding horse and chariot in a practical sense. It would be quite impossible to stand so straight and upright in a moving chariot without falling. But perhaps the artist did not even want to depict a charioteer in the arena, in the stadium, but an image of the human being upright and secure, a man in full control of drives, passions, instincts and desires—in short, a man in control of his 'horses'. For the observer the charioteer is an artistic symbol of the human being as such. In everyday life we are all at times overwhelmed by our instincts and passions and dragged along by them, but we are not free when this occurs.

The power and stamina of the 'horses' can vary. If, so to speak, we are thrown off the chariot, we will of course know that we are no longer in control. Some horses are temperamental and go their own way, even if they do not throw us. We may also not always realize that the reins have slipped from our grasp when we are surrounded by a pleasant landscape. We may not even feel out of control, and yet we are not the master and thus need to increase our conscious awareness in order to lead the horses.

Eugene Ionesco wrote the following words in his diary: 'It seems to me that I am not identical with my passions. I am someone who passionately yearns for another ego.'

What then enables us to be a charioteer rather than a passenger? At times two horses may pull in different directions, each neutralizing the movement of the other or until one gives way to the stronger pull of the other. Feelings can be passionate. They can graduate from very hot to very cold, and they can indeed become so overwhelmingly strong that they pull us under altogether. We lose track of ourselves. Forgetting oneself is not in the same league with selflessness. In forgetting ourselves we become passive victims. Selflessness means active participation. In the latter case the charioteer holds the reigns firmly and gets to where he wants to go, though he may have to sacrifice his selfish instincts in favour of aims he feels to be right.

Contemplation, reflection and thinking are tools which can lift us out of the pit of having forgotten ourselves. Beyond the instinctive patterns, feelings and emotions, we are also directed by ideas and precepts, which evolve from the lessons of life. Given circumstances evoke different feelings in each of us. We each have our own ideas and precepts to deal with, with their varying motivating force and impact. Some people have a lot of ideas but not enough stamina to do anything with them. Others have few ideas but carry them out with power and persistence. Among politicians we find notable examples of both sorts.

We are not always aware of the fact that our ideas, precepts and goals have a tendency to become guiding principles for our actions. If I often find myself saying, 'Now I will do what pleases me most,' this may slowly become a principle of action which moves me to say, 'Wherever possible I will do what gives me the greatest pleasure.' In this way ideas become principles, though of course not all our decisions are based on such principles.

As mentioned earlier, we are not always aware of our principles and precepts. Many people act unknowingly on the principle of the greatest possible pleasure. We might for instance want to help someone without knowing that our hidden agenda is self-gratification. If we offer a gift we may do so in the subconscious hope that the person who receives it will appreciate us more than before. Our desire for personal gratification is a past master at hiding behind the screen of altruism in the depths of our souls, though of course there are many who know well that their striving for personal happiness is the motivation.

What is it that makes us happy? Certainly, the answer will vary greatly from person to person. One seeks wealth and power connected with it. A second wants to lead a modest and healthy life. A third wants to be blameless in order to gain a place in heaven. All three act on the same principle. Things become more complicated when the direct road to happiness is blocked and a detour must be chosen. We can take the state of Israel as an example. Certain Israeli politicians want to live in peaceful coexistence with the neighbouring Arab states, foremost with the Palestinians. The Foreign Ministry of Israel has accepted as valid the thought that a healthy and prosperous neighbour will be a non-aggressive one. Thus, on the premise that a strong Syrian agriculture may pave the way to future peaceful coexistence, Israel is helping Syria with its vast projects of irrigation in the desert. Here again the goal is the happiness of the state of Israel. The principle of pursuing Israel's happiness and prosperity has cleverly and practically been combined with the happiness and prosperity of the neighbouring state.

We must admit that actions based on drives and instincts can be controlled by principles and ideas. Feelings of anger and the desire for revenge can be held in check by the overriding desire for personal happiness. For although strong feelings may call forth spontaneous and reckless impulses, the charioteer will firmly grasp the reigns of his emotional horses knowing that the end result would be disastrous to himself if he failed to do so. All the same it is a question whether we are free when we act on the principle of the pursuit of our own happiness. Are we truly comfortable within ourselves when we have our own advantage in mind, in this case our own happiness? Or do we put up with the feeling of discomfort for the sake of the end result? And if we do that, have we really made a free decision, one we want to do rather than put up with?

Now the pursuit of happiness is not by any means the only motivating force behind thought-directed actions. Other ideas are available, among them moral commands which can be the reins as well as the whips for our instinctive drives. The Ten Commandments in the Bible are the best known moral laws in the Western world. But do we act and decide freely when we follow them? In earlier centuries they exerted considerable power and were a great support for many people who wrestled with their emotions. Yet the Ten Commandments can sometimes lead to immense inner conflicts. We may consider for instance what happens when we suddenly develop a deep affection for someone while we are, at the same time, in another partnership. It puts us suddenly into a very difficult situation. Moral discernment is here quite clear: 'You shall not be disloyal'. But what can now arise is an agonizing conflict between our deeply felt inclinations on the one side and the demands of morality on the other. Which side is right? When do we act freely in such a case? Do we act freely when we give way to the passions of love, and throw the moral commandment overboard? For those who are firmly rooted in moral precepts the answer is easy: 'We are not at all free when we give in to a forbidden passion.' A powerful sympathy has thrown us off the chariot and is dragging us along. Morality demands that we overcome our passionate attachment. But even if we take up this standpoint, has not the subjugation of our feelings something brutal about it? Why, we may argue, is the attraction and love for the other person so despicable that it has to be suppressed at all costs? Has the attraction no justification in itself? True, passions and inclinations may run away with us, but merely suppressing them does not free us. In the one case passion overpowers morality, in the other morality smothers our feelings and affections. Real freedom can be found in neither course of action.

It would be hard to find another thinker who wrestled more intensely with this issue than Friedrich Schiller. Schiller's sympathies were on the side of strict moral accountability. In his opinion every person should in the last resort willingly prefer morality over passion. But even though Schiller felt that morality was the more worthy choice, he also did not see it as the ideal.

There is a cruel element in the suppression of such a passion as love. After all, human beings have been endowed with feelings and emotions as well as reason and morality. By devaluing either, something is taken away from human nature. Schiller pointed out that even if morality wins the battle over passions and inclinations, victory does not mean lasting peace. For, he said, 'the vanquished enemy can rise again, only reconciliation can really render him harmless'. In other words, the cause for enmity has to be eliminated for good to ensure that the suppressed passions will not begin to lead a secret life of their own and poison ours.

In antiquity we find an impressive relief sculpture from the time of the widespread Mithras religion, the *Vanquisher of the Bull* (see the picture below). We see a warrior who wrestles with a bull, overcomes and kills it. Two torchbearers stand on either side of the warrior, one with his torch held aloft, the other with it pointing downwards. The relief tells us that before the bull, the representative of untamed human passions, is overcome, the light of reason is pulled into the nether regions to serve our lower needs. After the bull has been slain, however, the light of reason enlightens human thoughts and feelings. It points upwards.

There is a vast difference between the charioteer who is in command of his horses and the warrior who overcomes and kills the bull. Schiller's ideal was without doubt the

charioteer. We can be sure that he himself often wrestled with his inner 'bull' without ever being quite satisfied with the result. He sought for a balance between the two opposing forces within human beings, a balance that makes inner freedom possible, for Schiller was convinced that 'the vanquished enemy can rise again and only a real reconciliation can render him harmless'.

How do we go about the task of 'reconciling the enemy'? We have taken a step forward with the discovery that the entire range of feelings, be they of sympathy or antipathy, have their valid and integral place in human nature. In order to reconcile them we have to get to know them. The feeling of sympathy, for instance, tells us something and it is up to us to interpret the message—which is not so easy. If we misinterpret the inner message of our feelings we run into problems. Drives and desires want above all to be satisfied and are past masters at hiding their true nature behind a smokescreen. They use our thinking faculties for their own purposes in order to justify their existence. They are very misleading and stoke the fires of conflict between people, often leaving behind a heap of destroyed relationships. Feelings in general do not easily or immediately reveal their true meaning and significance, nor is it easy for us to know how we ought to deal with and understand them. We best approach them with caution and clear thinking, until they reveal their true and rightful purpose, namely, to be intermediaries in human relationships. In the middle of an emotional storm it will not be easy to see and think clearly, just as churning waters will not mirror the surrounding landscape as well as a placid lake. Once we have managed, however, to creatively integrate the message which is alive in our feelings we will find that, surprisingly enough, we can do justice to both our moral and our emotional side. Schiller worked with the insight that in order 'to render the enemy harmless' one needs a sense for the artistic, and he had his own ideas on what 'artistic' meant. As a poet he found it at times impossible to mould certain ideas and poetic materials into the form he had in mind. His creativity was blocked. The same occasionally happened to Goethe, who was Schiller's friend. Goethe had, at one time, an interesting and challenging story which he wanted to present in the form of an epos (a story in verses) but he encountered difficulties. In the end he gave up and handed the whole package, ideas and all, to Schiller. Schiller in turn found the story unsuitable for an epos but saw that it had all the ingredients of a drama. So he moulded Goethe's idea into the well-known and well-loved drama *William Tell*.

Feelings belong to the internal raw materials for which we have to find the right form and contour. Seen in this light, emotions and passions are neither unreasonable nor immoral. If we patiently hone our creative sensibilities we will discover in time their inner reasoning and value. The artist in us becomes a charioteer who does not have to stop and wrestle with an untamed bull. He can channel and control his emotions because he is aware of their true nature and relevance. Here we have an image of what it means to act in the arena of freedom.

There are other areas still in which our pursuit of freedom is impeded by moral precepts and commandments. Schiller, who maintained that moral laws should always be valued more highly than actions based on instincts and desires, never mentioned why this should be so. What reasons can we find for accepting them? Or better, why should we make the laws of morality our own? Why do some if not all of them pertain to us?

About one hundred years ago the philosopher Friedrich Nietzsche caused a sensation when he voiced such thoughts, and began to search for the inner justification of moral axioms and laws. People were appalled. It was thought that the attempt to go into the origins of morality would be tantamount to undermining and destroying its foundation. In Nietzsche's case such people were not wholly wrong. But why ask the question at all? The likely answer is that when we do so we notice that by following moral precepts we still follow a

non-transparent authority. When we were children we heard
of these Commandments daily and were brought up to heed
them: you shall not lie, you shall not steal, you shall keep
faith with others, and so on. Perhaps we were punished for
breaking them in one way or another. Perhaps we were told
that these Commandments were given to mankind by God.
To our parents this was reason enough to keep them. In the
end we became used to them and accepted them. And yet we
wonder still whether our acceptance makes them true and
meaningful. It is our subconscious longing for freedom that
makes us wonder, or maybe even our conscious longing and
seeking. 'Moral laws say that lying is something bad and
wrong and that one should not lie. But can this fact be
recognized and understood for itself, or do I just accept it? If
I merely accept it, perhaps because I have grown up from
childhood with this belief and know no other, then I am not
really free.' Even if commandments have been given by an
individual human being, or originate from God, or if they
have been set up by society and have become tradition, I am
adhering each time to an external authority when I accept
these laws and try to follow them. This is so even in the
special case where the commands are not prescribed from
outside but speak from within as the voice of conscience.

Our own conscience can be a powerful authority. It usually
appears as warning or admonishment. But if we follow our
own conscience it does not always mean that we act morally.
People have committed the most gruesome crimes yet
maintained that their conscience was clear. It has been said
that such criminals have lost touch with their conscience, that
they do not even hear the small voice within. And yet it can
be argued that even if I listen to the voice of conscience and
act morally, I still listen to an authority. Though this
authority speaks within me, it is not myself that speaks. It
speaks to me and the 'it' is not 'I'. Never mind that it speaks
important truths, it is not I who speaks them and therefore I
follow a voice that is not identical with myself. At times the
voice of my conscience is so loud that I cannot but submit to

its command. It is quiet after it has had its way, but have I done what I wanted to do freely?

Not many people dare to ask such a question. In those who do, there lives a strong desire to be free, to be *self*-responsible and no one's servant. Are we free when we follow our conscience? In the last resort we probably have to say: 'No'. We follow a power that is not ourselves, be it ever so moral. As servants of conscience we bring forth moral actions but we are not free in them.

So far so good. I have determined that I do not have to follow the dictates of my own conscience. But is it possible to do the bidding of conscience because I want to follow it? Can I follow the voice of conscience because I want to do it? That is of course possible. I can follow the voice of conscience because I find that it makes sense to do so rather than feeling impelled to my actions. If I can be convinced to act because the message, the intent of my conscience is meaningful and valid, I act because I myself want to act. In that case my own intentions and those of my conscience are one and the same. I act in accordance with my insight.

We have now reached an important stage in our progress towards freedom when we base our actions upon insight into the reason for a commandment. It matters little whether we are faced with an injunction from outer authorities or whether our own conscience is the demanding voice. We act because our insight into the nature of the regulation is the guiding light. Speed limits for example will initially make us feel less than free, since they restrict our freedom of movement. We may follow them because, as law-abiding citizens, we acknowledge the authority of the government, and further because we do not want to incur a fine. Or we may deem the speed limit meaningful and justified. The reason may be that 200,000 people world-wide die each year from traffic accidents, the main cause being excessive speed. High speeds also increase harmful emissions. With such thoughts we see that speed limits have good reason and to the extent that we cultivate such ideas, speed signs lose their character of making us unfree. We obey the signs, no longer from a belief in authority or from fear of penalties, but from an understanding of their reasons.

We can deal in a similar manner with all regulations, even with the input of our own conscience. If we understand the legitimacy of parental rules, for instance, and come to identify with them by completely thinking them through, we will stop rebelling against them.

In the same way too we can try to understand the commands of morality and of conscience. Here we meet again the question whether moral precepts can be established only on the basis of authority. One can, however, express it differently. Can we see through the content of moral precepts just as clearly as we can grasp a mathematical relationship? If we can do so they will lose their air of authority and we can rely on their internal logic instead. Can we establish the proposition 'you should not lie' just as firmly as the proposition that the sum total of angles in a triangle is 180°? If this were not possible for us, why do we thus obey the command? Certainly it would not be from insight. It would be about the same as if the statement $2 + 5 = 7$ were to be accepted on good faith, or because society had agreed to it, or on the authority of those who advocated this proposition. Imagine the face of a young child that has been taught that $5 + 2 = 7$. It believes what the teacher has said and learns it by heart. Now imagine the shining face of the same child when it discovers that it can understand the logic behind the statement that $5 + 2 = 7$, and can test the logic for itself without relying on the authority of the teacher.

With regard to moral laws are we not often in the same position as the small child when it learns of a mathematical truth it does not yet understand? Are we not usually at a loss when we are asked about the establishment of moral precepts? In the history of philosophy philosophers have made various attempts to develop the basis for moral ideas and their logical reasons. One of them, Immanuel Kant, looked at the moral guidelines as they presented themselves to him in the context of the society he lived in and within his own conscience. He then sought to find the underlying moral principles. In other words, he sought for their universal and undeniable common denominator. 'What is the common principle of all moral laws known to us?' He answered this question with a formula that has since become famous: 'Always act so that the basis of your action may be valid for all.'

Kant believed that this thought represented the basic principle of all possible moral commandments. But how can we understand it? A maxim or principle is in itself so right that it fits all possible scenarios. Let us look again at the maxim: 'I should never lie'. According to Kant's formula a maxim is morally 'good' if it can be generalized; more exactly if the generalized principle and the personal principle do not contradict. So for instance if the principle 'I should not lie' is true for myself, it must not contradict what Kant called the 'universal law,' which is: 'All men should not lie'. This means that if it is valid for me it is valid for everyone, without it giving rise to a logical contradiction. It is not contradictory for me to say that I should not lie and at the same time say that everyone else should not lie. We now reverse the law to prove its universal application by saying: 'I want to lie.' According to Kant we cannot demand for ourselves the privilege of lying without granting it to everyone, and that voids the meaning of the principle. We can easily see why this is so. If I lie, I do so in order to profit at the cost of others. If everyone else lies, the wished for effect is made void, it is logical nonsense. Kant saw this as the proof of the self-defeating nonsense of immorality, while the morally 'good' principles never lead to such contradictions.

Inherent in this sequence of thoughts is the insight that immoral actions and decisions are not logical. Immoral actions are anti-social because the harmony and wholeness of the people involved—two or more people are always involved—is not served. Immoral and illogical decisions are as logically nonsensical as mathematical errors. I cannot want to live and prosper within a society whose foundations I want to undermine at the same time. I can, of course, act immorally but in that case my action is not logical. I only refuse to see it as such.

Such were Kant's thoughts in essence. Through them we can come a step closer to understanding moral laws. We do not wish to get into logical contradictions with our actions. Insight into the justification of the commandments replaces the external authority. 'Thou shalt...' becomes: 'I will...'

Right now we might be tempted to counter: 'Why should we want to act logically? Why should we not follow our whims and act illogically? Why should we prefer one decision over another?' The simple answer is: 'A true insight speaks for itself. Nothing else is needed unless you are meandering through a labyrinth of theories. If you have found through thought and insight good reasons for your actions, you will act accordingly and not do the opposite. Once insight has been gained into the reasons for moral principles, they will occupy the same position as axioms do towards mathematical theorems. Whoever endeavours to understand moral guidelines will try to find their corresponding axioms.'

In the history of philosophy we can find quite a number of other principles or axioms besides those of Kant. These axioms are transparent and can be the guide for nearly all our actions One of them is the idea that we ought to act for the maximum happiness of the greatest number of people, a principle which Jeremy Bentham conceived. That is, 'the greatest good for the greatest number'. If we act upon this formula, we will achieve a high degree of freedom. Nothing propels us other than our own insight into the principle—no drives, no instincts, no moral laws. We act on the basis of an ideal principle which we ourselves have chosen.

With this result have we now reached our goal? Have we finally found the answer to the question of freedom? To act freely is to act on the basis of insight? But are there experiences which contradict this? Are there not instances where we have made great efforts to understand a principle, finally agreed with it and yet felt not wholly free in acting in accordance with it? Why is that? One has acted on the basis of insight but not felt free in doing so. Such experiences cast doubt on our conclusion; it may be theoretically valid but not convincing in practice. It is now important to go more closely into such experiences and seek their cause.

Different people take hold of insights in different ways. An insight which has a theoretical character is mostly ineffective and does not lead to the feeling of freedom as a matter of course. On the contrary. To follow it can be laborious and even irksome. Sometimes we may even feel more free in following our own wishes in opposition to a theoretical insight, though in this case we are deceived in believing it has anything much to do with a genuine feeling of freedom. If we do as we wish, the wish is silenced, much as the feeling of hunger is stilled after we have eaten. If we are no longer hungry we are freed from hunger. If the wish no longer bothers us, we are free of it and have a feeling of liberation. But as soon as insight and wish begin to battle within us, we are like the charioteer who is losing control of his horses. He gives the horses their lead because he is tired of their obstinate pull and feels liberated thereby. The other way round we can also have the experience that a real insight hardly ever opposes the healthy instincts and desires of the human being. What our example shows, however, is that a theoretical insight is not definitely stronger than the soul's desires. And it is in this realm that people differ. History has shown us people who loved their ideals and their ideal-based insights so much that many of their own urges and persuasions were silenced. Other people have such insights that are pale and hollow for lack of inner persuasion. For them it is hard work indeed to act on them.

G.E. Lessing has portrayed the struggle of one such character in his drama *Nathan der Weise* ('Nathan the Wise') Nathan is a Jew who lives in Jerusalem during the time of the Crusades. His seven children have been killed by marauding Crusaders. Nathan is utterly devastated by the loss. While he is weeping, mourning in deepest sorrow, a passing rider places a small bundle on his doorstep. In the bundle is a Christian baby. When Nathan sees the baby he is for a moment torn by a most violent inward struggle. His Jewish religion has taught him to take 'an eye for an eye, a tooth for a tooth', but Nathan himself has achieved the understanding that love and readiness to help are worthier impulses than hatred and revenge. This extreme situation puts him to the test and later on he relates how in this moment he called out to himself, saying: 'Practise what you have long understood to be the right thing to do.' Nathan follows his own ideals and takes the Christian child into his house. In the course of time he has thoughts which shed an unexpected light on his situation, for he realizes that a kind destiny gave the child into his care, as a compensation for the loss of his own children. The cause for revenge was transformed into a blessing. 'In the place of my own seven I have at least the one.' In this scene Lessing points out how theoretical understanding and practical application are two different things. The theoretical insight has to prove its value in reality, much like the potential for growth in a seed which manifests when the conditions of light and warmth are right. The reader gains the impression that when barren, theoretical insights are transformed they become the fertile soil on which a new life can grow. Nathan's inner struggle for morality created something like warmth, his insight the light and his pain the fertile ground. Having acted from such insight leaves him feeling happy and blissfully free. We can recognize in this example that an insight must first be brought to life if it is to make possible the feeling of freedom.

In our modern society innumerable insights exist, but few of them come to life in human minds. Indeed one might say that we live in an age filled with innumerable insights that lead nowhere. Theories abound in heads but are not taken up by hearts so as to lead into corresponding actions. A great deal for instance is known about the destruction of our environment, but apart from a few individuals or single groups no one does anything much about it. The case is rather as described before. We do not feel free when we follow our own insights, whereas on the contrary it imposes unacceptable limitations. The Nathans in modern life are few and far between. It is rare to find people whose insights live and inspire their actions.

What can we do so that our ideas become more than brilliant but uncomfortable structures in our heads? What can we do to give them a home in our hearts so that they lend fire and enthusiasm to our deeds?

4.   The Human Being

The light in the eyes of a child is bright when it has understood an arithmetical relationship, but it is ever so much brighter when it learns how to discover the facts for itself and that all is part of an encompassing, ordered whole governed by law. If we apply this picture to human action in general, we are led to a higher level of freedom—the level of our own moral invention. This highest stage of experience is at the core of Rudolf Steiner's book *The Philosophy of Spiritual Activity*.

We have seen that acting on the basis of insight into a moral command constitutes a high degree of freedom. We are made unfree neither by instincts nor passions, nor by moral prescriptions. We follow a principle because we have understood its content and have made it the guideline for our actions. But we have come across the principle, it was already there. Then we have grasped it understandingly just as a small child has understood the solution of a problem. But we have not invented it. Why, however, should it not also be possible to create or invent moral ideas? How can we do that? Are we to become inventors of morality? Must one not be endowed with the mind of a genius to be an inventor? Not all of us are as brilliant as Carl Friedrich Gauss who was able to discover grandiose mathematical formulae. Rudolf Steiner's reply is: 'Not everyone is a moral inventor, a moral genius, but everyone can become one.' There is something liberating and grandiose in such thoughts: 'I don't have to be static, I can become, I can evolve into a genius. As I am, I am perhaps still hampered and limited, but I have it in me to discover moral ideas, and to practise until the genius in me awakens.'

The inventor or discoverer of a moral idea is, in more ways than one, different from the person who follows the guidelines of moral commandments or his own conscience, even if the action has its basis in insight. Moral guidelines and precepts are rigid and immovable. They are valid, independent of the situation. If, for instance, I act according to the precept of the greatest good for the greatest number, I am bound to it in all possible circumstances, because I have to ask myself every time if the greatest number of people will truly benefit from my decision. Of course we will in time become more adept at being purveyors of common happiness. Since principles and laws are always valid, regardless of the circumstance, the character of our actions and decisions will be static. However, a moral idea we invent does not have to be valid for all possible cases, only for the particular instance we are currently dealing with. And for each situation in life a quite individual moral idea can be found. Let us imagine a specific problem between two people. What we need to find is a morally valid idea befitting the situation and the problem. And this is something different from knowing at the start, here, say, the principles of loyalty or of the greatest good for the greatest number of people are involved.

To act in such a way may be irritating and disquieting for people who position themselves firmly on the side of moral laws and commands. They will think that nothing good will ensue if the commandment of loyalty is not absolutely obeyed. They will be afraid the search for a special moral idea will be used to justify infidelity. Yet such arguments only prove that the concept of moral ideas has not been understood. To show that their fear is unfounded we again use an earlier comparison.

A mathematical discovery expands the scope of mathematics *per se*, but it must always be in full concordance with all other mathematical laws and axioms already known and never contradict or exclude any of them. The world of mathematics is a spiritual entity of mutually interrelated principles into which non-conforming discoveries cannot be absorbed. In like manner the moral world consists of a network in which various moral models do not exclude nor contradict one another. For this reason Rudolf Steiner wrote in his book *The Philosophy of Spiritual Activity*, 'Acting out of freedom (one based on the discovery of a moral idea) does not exclude the moral laws; it includes them, but shows itself to be on a higher level than those actions which are merely dictated by such laws.' A moral idea, individually discovered, is worth more than a moral decree and cannot be at odds with general moral precepts. Should there be a conflict we must either blame it on a defective moral decree or on a defective moral idea. A 'good' moral idea 'is one that harmonizes with the world as a whole'.

Here we see the difference between an idea that has been created to solve a certain problem and one that is predetermined. The resulting action will in the former case be flexible, in the latter it will follow a given format. It is also possible to discover many moral ideas through ongoing spiritual activity, so that when faced with a problem we can call upon a number of possible solutions and choose the one that we like best. The free spirit chooses it and puts it into action because it loves the idea it has found, just as every discoverer of spiritual realities loves his own discovery. A relationship of the heart is established between the free spirit and the morally created idea. While inner aversions may have to be overcome when a theoretical insight moves us into action, the inventor of moral ideas has no such problem. The discovery is loved wholeheartedly. There is no gap between theoretical understanding and practical application.

Every person will come to find different moral ideas. This is the second big difference. Actions based on general principles tend to render people spiritually uniform. Where everyone acts according to the same principle, spiritual habits are uniformly the same. People who try to rise above principles and norms become creative individuals. They are inventors and discoverers of moral ideas, though they may live under different circumstances and have different ideas. The world of ideas is open to everyone, and our individuality will be marked by the sum total of effective ideas we have selected to work within us.

People who are morally productive, those who strive to create moral ideas, can have a remarkable experience. Their creative activity will open the door to the reality of their own ego, very gently at first and in time more and more widely. It will evoke a feeling of deep delight in recognizing that this is my true I. I myself am the one who brought these ideas forth and I love them. They will find out that this I, the creator of such ideas, can grow in inward scope and substance. Whereas before they had felt their ego-being but vaguely, they now come to experience it through their own creative efforts. It is a blissful experience that in its wake may kindle soul-moving, soul-elevating thoughts. They begin to realize the full potential of what it means to be human. They realize that they are not really a human being unless they strive towards fulfilment.

Others without such an experience may feel the above sentence meaningless or even repugnant. To most people a human being is a human being, a member of the human race from the moment of birth until death, much as a sheep dog is a sheep dog from puppyhood on until it dies. A little child to them is as much a human being as any adult; it only becomes older and more grown up. This thought is valid, but only when we look at it from the outside. There is, of course, no need to argue whether every person is a human being. It would indeed be silly to doubt it. But from the viewpoint of our inner life the picture changes.

We find out that we have to realize or fulfil ourselves first of all. Becoming human means more than ageing—it means awareness and development of our potential to become a free spirit. Once we truly experience ourselves as the creator of ideas, we learn to look at ourselves as we really are. Everything else, our thinking and emotional habits will become side-effects whose sense and meaning will become clear at a later date. We find out at the same time that the creative ego can become powerful and great whereas it is as yet small and underdeveloped. Within the circumference of this ego I find myself as human being. It is who I am and as such I want to grow and become more and more real. Now I see who I am as idea and it is I who must help this idea to become real, step by step. In this respect human beings differ from all other nature-created beings. Inherent in the seed of a tree is the building plan for the mature tree—the idea. Nature sees to it that this particular idea will unfold into a real tree. This is where human beings differ. Only the individual self can unfold its spiritual 'building plan', its 'idea', namely, to become a free spirit. It cannot be any other way because a free spirit who is not self-creative is also not free.

As far as the creative free spirit is concerned, we have to keep in mind that the idea of the human being can be comprehended in various forms, of which thinking is only one. Artistically creative people experience ideas they bring forth out of themselves in colours, music and shapes, in movement or inner images. Mozart was one who grasped his ideas in the form of melodies and harmonies and found himself in and through his music. The listener will hear the unmistakable style of Mozart and recognize his musical ideas even if the music is heard for the first time. The wealth and riches of Mozart's creative ideas in his later works is truly astonishing. It has been said of Beethoven that in his music there weave and play more profound thoughts than in the greatest conceptually formulated philosophies. The ideas of the spiritual world can thus be grasped and communicated in varied ways.

If we now set out to put a moral idea into practice, we need more than just our love for it—we also need imagination. We can, for example, imagine an inventor who has conceived the idea of a vehicle that can drive up and down stairs evenly without bumping at every step. But he does not yet know how to construct it. The mere idea of a 'stairway vehicle' does not tell him how to do so. To develop the building plans he must have the technical know-how. So now he uses imagination to draw up a practical and detailed plan for a vehicle which does not yet exist. Moreover, he cannot let his imagination run wild but must focus it clearly and precisely on the problem before him. A practical and productive inventor needs a practical and productive imagination that takes the idea beyond the theoretical stage.

The same is true for human actions in general. We need the right kind of imagination in order to make our ideas work. Rudolf Steiner speaks in his book *The Philosophy of Spiritual Activity* of the need for 'moral imagination'. It is tempting for someone with moral ideas alone to start preaching and telling everyone what should, could or must be done without suggesting specifically how they can be done. But if the moral idea is to be of any practical value a practical imagination is needed in addition. Mere preaching is not productive. Nor is the inventor wise who applies for a patent for his stair-driving vehicle before he has come up with a detailed technical plan. It is possible, however, that if we ourselves lack the practical know-how someone else can fill the gap. If we have good moral ideas but lack moral imagination we can try to find someone who has, so that a fruitful collaboration may result.

Real life examples are readily found. I may for instance meet a man who has all sorts of problems and the moral idea may come up in me that might alleviate his difficulties. Since it is my idea and impulse to help, I will do so with all my heart. But this does not mean that I know right away what to do. At this point my moral imagination must be called on to devise a practical plan.

Another story comes to mind, this time of a man in conflict with the law. He had often been in trouble before because he could not tame his errant drives, but he finally managed to find a job as a foreman in a city firm. He had been given another chance. But as before, he behaved improperly towards his colleagues and it was clear that he would soon be dismissed or even go to prison. The personnel manager realized that the man had to be dismissed, that indeed he had no choice in the matter since the law demanded it, as well as the other employees. And yet he wanted to help the unfortunate man. That was his moral idea. But the idea alone was not enough and, since he did not know how to help, he asked the man to meet him for a talk. In the course of the conversation he urged the distraught man to tell him about something he really liked to do. The man mumbled that he was very fond of animals. Then, after this meeting, the manager had a talk with the director of the local zoo who agreed to take the man on probation as an assistant keeper. Some weeks later the director of the zoo called to thank the manager for his referral, stating that rarely had he met a man more capable of dealing with animals and that no trace of his former problems remained. Work on a fulfilling and satisfying task had blown them away.

This example can teach us several things. For one, it makes clear the difference between moral ideas and moral imagination. Further, it shows how action based on self-discovered moral ideas does not conflict with the family of moral laws but includes and transcends them. The man was dismissed as required by law but at the same time he was given the help he needed. Finally, the little story elucidates a basic problem underlying all moral-philosophical examples, namely, that it is not necessarily a true example of moral ingenuity. We cannot truly know whether the manager acted from compassion or on the commandment 'love your neighbour', or on the principle of the greatest happiness for the greatest number. In other words, it does not necessarily prove the presence of a novel moral idea. Since this is a valid objection, the question arises: 'Could any one example really convince us?' To know the answer we would have to know at least the motivation behind the action. But even then, even if we knew the inner motivation, a critical thinker might infer self-deception. Another question is whether we really need examples? We can only judge our own motivations and that is already difficult enough. More fruitful than the analysis of other people's motivations is the effort to become an inventor of moral ideas and to beware of self-deceptions. Perhaps Rudolf Steiner had good reasons for not giving any examples for moral imagination in his book *The Philosophy of Spiritual Activity*. Indeed, are not examples themselves in contradiction to the idea of unique moral inventions?

Moral imagination enables us to put our moral ideas into practice. Without moral imagination the latter would remain mere spiritual models with unused inherent powers. If we want to take hold of life and apply our ideas to it, we need, besides moral imagination, as profound a knowledge as possible of the sphere in which we want to work, as well as its laws. Much as the mechanic needs sound technical experience and knowledge of mechanics in order to get his vehicle to roll up the stairs, so does everyone need to know the given realities of their chosen field of work for moral imagination to be successful. A kindergarten teacher needs to know about the developmental stages of young children if the work is to benefit the children rather than damage them. If, for instance, kindergarten teachers know that children live and grow by imitating the adults in their environment, they will want to keep it in mind as a basis for their work at all times.

Rudolf Steiner calls *moral technique* the knowledge of the inner laws and functions of life's realities, in which we aim to work and create by using our moral ideas and imagination. While even the best of moral intentions are impractical unless they are attuned to the realities of life, the 'moral technician' has these realities in mind and acts accordingly.

Great and powerful ideas require the practical help and knowledge of many people in order to succeed. One such great idea is Rudolf Steiner's insight into the threefold nature of the human being as a foundation for the further evolution of human kind. It is moral imagination which led from here to the threefold nature of the state in its spiritual, legal and economic life. But an enormous amount of detailed knowledge in all these areas of life will be required if everyday life is to be transformed in the spirit of these powerful ideas, and innumerable people will have to contribute their initiative and knowledge to bring them to reality. But the work will also enable those involved to evolve new moral techniques and to realize in turn that their own insights will become wider and deeper.

This book has been written to prepare the reader for the study of *The Philosophy of Spiritual Activity*, which Rudolf Steiner published in 1894. There he used the term *moral intuition*, to describe what we have here called 'moral idea'. Moral intuition is the thought-content of moral thinking or more exactly the form in which moral ideas and concepts initially enter the human mind. Human thinking lives in a world of ideas and concepts. By way of thinking we take our ideas and concepts from this world, where they become part of our consciousness. In this form, namely those ideas which live in human consciousness, Rudolf Steiner calls them intuitions.

We have now obtained an overview of three mutually enhancing levels out of which the free human being can act:

1) Moral intuition—moral ideas which we have made and loved.
2) Moral imagination—that transforms our moral intuitions into specific mental pictures.
3) Moral technique—which makes available the detailed knowledge of those areas in life we want to work in.

Together these three realms contribute to the form of inner freedom possible for the human being. By grasping moral intuitions and through our love for them we become free spirits. By means of moral imagination and moral technique, inner freedom becomes a reality in everyday life. It is the latter two, moral imagination and moral technique, which are sometimes misunderstood. The love for a moral intuition has united whole groups in the service of its cause. Yet the lack of moral imagination or moral technique has rendered the intuitions more or less ineffective. The result is often sorrow, stagnation, bitterness or even resignation. And when we become aware of such problems we are face to face with the next important question: 'How can we develop the necessary faculties?'

5. The Path

From all that has been said so far, one thing is clear. Whether the human being is free or not is a wrong or fuzzy way of putting the question. If, however, we want an answer in this form then we must at least enquire more exactly what is meant by the words 'human being'. Is it those who live today all over the earth in such countless numbers? Or human beings in the sense of what each of us can become? In the first case we would have to say that no one is really free, or only to a very limited extent. For who would say of themselves that they are free in all their actions? Is not rather the opposite true, that free actions are very much the exception?

In the second case we can now reply as follows. Within every human being there lies the potential to be free, to become human in the full sense. As we are, we are not free. But we all have the higher human being within us as seed, as potential. Nevertheless it is only we who can develop this into a reality as we liberate ourselves more and more from the confused mass of unfree actions and rise to the level of the higher man.

Yet freedom does not come of itself. It does not fall into our lap. Either we work at it to make freedom a reality or it remains a mere possibility. But this last basically contradicts our own nature; it is unnatural. In all of us there lives the yearning to be free and to become more than we are at present. And here lies the apparent paradox. What is natural does not happen naturally for human beings. Each of us must produce what is natural by our own efforts, namely, the capacity for free action. And this productive process appears in a double aspect. It is a gigantic task hardly to be measured. Indeed, it is the most difficult of all. On the other hand, it can be worked at in various stages and in various ways, so that each step forward brings to reality something of the full human being who, at the same time, is always potentially a free being.

The fulfilment of the human being is thus only possible as a result of effort and practice. In his *Philosophy of Spiritual Activity* Rudolf Steiner clearly expresses this but does not give it prominence. In later lectures where he speaks about his book, considerable emphasis is indeed given to the path towards inner freedom as one of training and discipline. We will therefore take another look at some of the forms of non-freedom described earlier and examine to what extent the idea of freedom is made clearer through them.

The lack of freedom which Albrecht Haushofer wrestled with in his *Moabit Sonnets* has two sources. The first are the reflex type of actions arising from instincts, desires and passions, and the second are the actions that spring from principles like personal benefit, moral commands and other basic precepts which we have gained as a result of insight. Moral intuition helps us overcome these little by little, but in the reality of everyday life some things stand in the way of moral intuition. One of these especially is our undisciplined and unfocused way of thinking. Moral intuitions are grasped through thinking, but the less disciplined and unhealthy our thinking is the more difficult it is to grasp and hold moral intuitions. In the normal state of affairs our thoughts are quite unconcentrated and jump around from one topic to the next. Impressions bombard our senses and lead our thoughts on a merry dance. Inner distractions do the same. Thus our thinking is far removed from what it is capable of achieving.

A first exercise will therefore be to learn to focus, to concentrate our thinking. Naturally we will not be able to do this all the time, but we can begin with shorter periods such as five minutes each day. Within these five minutes we consciously choose a topic, preferably one outside of our normal range, and allow our thoughts to dwell on it. It is best to begin with simple man-made objects, for instance a jug, and unfold a sequence of thoughts about it. We will soon find that all thoughts will focus on the *idea* of the jug, since man-made objects are the manifestations of functional ideas. The function of an object determines its make, material, production and history. Step by step, thought after thought, we think only on the subject 'jug'. If our thoughts stray we call them back. If we stray for instance in the direction of milk in the jug, the farmer, the cow, the barn and the last farm holiday, we think by association, which means that we are not thinking will-directed thoughts and are not free.

In the beginning it will be easy because a lot of ideas will occur to us. However, after two or three days things change. New thoughts are less abundant and the old ones are repeated. The original easy exercise becomes a difficult one, but right here we need to go on and overcome the apparent difficulty by deepening our thoughts. Then after one week the topic can be changed, or earlier if a dead end has been reached.

A simple exercise of this kind will slowly make our thoughts more subtle and pliable. If we notice this we will take joy in the exercise like a musician who enjoys practising because he sees he is making progress. Thought concentration will become more enjoyable as time goes on provided we do not give up after the first or second week. We school our will forces in the process, for we act on our own decisions and not because anyone coerces us.

Schooling the will, however, is not without pitfalls. If we miss a practice we are tempted to give it all up. But we should not become discouraged. If we stumble once, we pick ourselves up again. If we stumble ten times we pick ourselves up ten times until we have regained our joy in the concentration and certainty of thinking.

It is possible to supplement this exercise by adding another. Rudolf Steiner has mentioned in lectures that his *Philosophy of Spiritual Activity* can be used as a book for inner training. In reference to the ancient concept of 'catharsis' (purification), he explains the following: 'A person can go far towards a state of catharsis, for instance, if everything which stands in my book *The Philosophy of Spiritual Activity*, is inwardly worked through and experienced until the following feeling arises: "The book has been a stimulus for me, but I myself can now reproduce its thought-content out of myself''. If such is one's inner attitude—and it has been written with this use in mind—the student is like a virtuoso who plays the music strictly as the composer wrote it, but reproduces it in his own way. In such a case, the rigorous sequence of thoughts in the book can lead to a high degree of catharsis.'

In a practical sense it means, to begin with, that we learn by heart single chapters of the book, much as a virtuoso learns the music he is going to play. Naturally it is not meant that we learn all the pages by heart word for word, but the organization of the thought sequences. The musician learns by playing and practising the passages over and over again until he remembers the entire piece. Here we follow the trains of thoughts in the book and make them our own just as a musician treats his sheet music. In the end we will have the content at our disposal. Once a chapter has been mastered in this way we will notice as a side-effect that our thinking has become quicker, more flexible and agile. We will notice a definite change from the former rigidity and clumsiness of our thoughts. It also becomes easier to absorb other thoughts. The enlivening of our own thinking leads to a feeling of deep happiness and we get an inkling of what it means to really think. Those who have had this experience will vouch for the fact that their thinking has begun to be rejuvenated and that, even though the world has considered them intelligent before, they now know that their earlier thinking was a jumbled hotch-potch by comparison.

The above exercise can be done even if we have not yet understood important ideas in *The Philosophy of Spiritual Activity*. A musician too can learn a whole piece even if he has not yet mastered some of the passages.

The next level of the exercise then deals just with those thoughts that are difficult to understand. This should be briefly mentioned. The long inner struggle with unsolved questions waiting for an answer may resemble the torture of Tantalus, a mythological figure who stood up to his neck in water without being able to reach it and quench his thirst. In such a way problem questions from the book can face the student; one can read the thoughts without understanding them. The bliss when understanding dawns at last will make all the former pain worth while, and the light of understanding will also fall on further areas of the book. We no longer feel so markedly inadequate as before. This kind of practice will not be to everyone's taste, nor does it have to be. It is not to be thought of as having more value than other forms of practice on the path to inner freedom.

The one thing we discover for sure, however, is the fact that we can expand and develop our thinking capacity. Behind our normal everyday mode of thinking there lies a much more vigorous and powerful form whose development can become a necessity of life. Above all, we find we can rely on it and gain increasing confidence in it. It can become effective before we even realize it consciously. Particularly in times of difficulty, when calls are made on our moral imagination, it is possible to come closer to the source of living thinking. If we are, for instance, dissatisfied with the way we have acted in a conflict situation, it is helpful to use the evening or the next morning to reflect upon it all in peace and quiet. We try to see the whole objectively, as if from outside. If we were angry or furious, we try to let these feelings fall away and in their stead cultivate a feeling of calm. Into this feeling of calm we can now plant thoughts in preparation for moral imagination, which will come about if we separate the essential from the inessential. Once we have grasped what is important, we will be able to know how to act in the future. Quite often we just see to begin with the direction in which we ought to go, though no specific way of doing so. But once the impulse permeates us we will notice that it works within us through the night like a seed that begins to sprout, and the day will bring us positive ways of dealing with the issues. That is how imagination works in its early stages. It is called forth gently by inner tranquillity, while our thoughts dwell on the objective side of the problem. Then it becomes specific, and we will feel happy in our actions for they will be meaningful and contribute to a solution.

Alongside the 'exercises' in thinking, Rudolf Steiner introduces a further field for practice, namely, a schooling of the will. Note the difference between 'will' and 'wish', since we tend to take the one for the other in everyday usage. We often say 'I will' when we mean 'I wish I could'. Yet we do not consider someone strong willed who often says 'I will ...' without taking the necessary action. Such a person is wishful but not necessarily strong-willed. A strong-willed person acts out his intentions, for the will is a power that enables us to translate our ideas into actions. All of us can observe how strong or otherwise this power is and ask whether it can be strengthened further within ourselves. A weak will impedes our quest for freedom, indeed it is a form of unfreedom. If we want to do something but do not do it because our will is too weak, this means we are hindered and limited by a defective faculty. To that extent we are also not free. To a greater or lesser extent we all suffer today from this form of unfreedom, an insufficiently strong will. And if we take the time to consider why this should be so, we have only to look at the way people have lived during the past few generations, and especially at how children grew up.

People in our present-day culture have applied their impressive intelligence to technical means of reducing work and making it easy for themselves. It has long been a human dream to advance to the point where technical inventions can relieve us of manual labour. Aristotle, a philosopher in ancient Greece, already dreamed of a loom whose shuttle would run back and forth 'by itself', that is, by mechanical means. His dream and much more have become reality to an almost unimaginable degree in the industrial state. It is not our intention to discuss here the significance of modern technology or the point at which it changes from sense into nonsense. We will only take a brief look at the effects it has had on the development of human will. In the highly technologized Western world, children grow up from the youngest age with an awareness of how much can be achieved by pressing buttons. The press of a button is enough to turn on lights, heat the stove and warm the house. Doors open, stairs roll up or down carrying passengers, turning a key starts the car, which effortlessly conveys us from one place to the next without our having to walk. Children experience all this and are deeply affected by it. But what the child sees is only half the truth. Only much later will the child realize that behind each press of the button and its results there stands a vast amount of work and intelligence. And even then only a few people will ever get first-hand experience of a power station, manufacturing plant or even a coal mine.

This state of affairs need not here be judged or criticised, but we can well find it is one of the causes of our civilization's sickness—*unfreedom from weakness of will*. Deep within us lies the childhood impressions that everything must go at the push of a button. In adult life these re-emerge perhaps in the belief that environmental problems are not really problems at all. We can easily solve them. 'Put a filter in, take the dirt out, best of all at the push of a button.' But this is a great illusion to which we all more or less succumb today. The world of button pushing is not just a comfortable one but it also lames the will. This laming of will, however, not only constitutes a danger but also provides a great opportunity. On the one hand the danger consists in succumbing more and more to this paralysis so that in the extreme case we come to live in an armchair and regulate our whole life from such a position by means of computer and robot. On the other hand, the opportunity consists in consciously schooling the will-power that in earlier generations was, in a way, simply given to us.

Rudolf Steiner's will-exercise is deceptively simple. Each day we resolve to do one small thing, something we might not have done normally, and then do it. It need not be anything that really matters. For instance, we can resolve to clean our desk top every day at a certain time. The scope of the

cleaning is not important nor does it have to make much
sense. Even a rather meaningless act like tying a shoelace or
winding a watch at the same time every day will do. The
difficulty lies in doing the same thing at the same time every
day without fail.

It is usually quite easy to do for one week, but after four
weeks we can discover that the difficulty of doing even easy
tasks has meaning and purpose. After four weeks or more of
carrying out this exercise strictly and without a gap, we will
notice a small increase in our own will-power. In time we will
also be less inclined to put off things we do not like to do,
which we tend to postpone. We can even integrate them into
the exercise. If such should be our inclination, we are reaping
the first tangible fruit of the exercise. We can later enlarge
the scope of our self-chosen activities, but they must be done
likewise without fail. It is not a good idea to be too ambitious
at first or to choose too many activities. The will to enlarge
the scope of the exercise should grow out of its own success,
just as the musician will also practise difficult pieces more
readily once the first level has been mastered successfully.

Those who have been successful in doing this exercise and
its extensions have experienced its liberating effect. Will-
power, formerly idle and responding only to outer pressure,
is now more and more ready to spring into action from itself.
We are suddenly eager to organize our day's activities more
purposefully, and though we may initially tend to over-
estimate the tenacity of our will, in time we will get to know
what we can and cannot do. Our will assumes the role of a
master in its own house, where previously it was the lazy
servant. We learn to take charge of those acts and decisions
which we used to shun as burdensome and oppressive.

Here too the exercise described above has its own pitfalls.
It is possible that through pressure of unforeseen circumstances or through our own inattention we are sometimes
thrown off course. Firstly, this should not discourage us, and
secondly we can well settle in the meantime for an easier
exercise that takes perhaps less time. The main thing is not to

give up. Rudolf Steiner suggests a time-frame of four weeks for each of the exercises, thought concentration and will, where one or the other stands in the foreground. One begins a month of thinking exercises, then during the second month the will exercises come to the fore. A third exercise is added in the third month, by carrying out both parallel with each other, perhaps on a smaller scale. Moreover, it is easier to carry out the sequence of exercises in a weekly rhythm and then change over to a monthly rhythm.

If we take a moment now to look back at the possibility described above of developing moral imagination, we come across a difficulty that leads to a third type of exercise. This one addresses our feelings. Up to now we have used our thinking to separate the important from the unimportant elements which motivate our will, with a focus on the important elements only. But these at times are hard to fathom because they still tend to hide behind a smokescreen of emotions. How, though, do we silence our emotions? An example may suggest one way.

Let us say someone has offended me so that I am upset and feel attacked without due cause. At the beginning of the exercise these feelings may re-emerge more or less strongly. But I can now realize that it always depends on me whether I feel offended or not. Even if the offence was intended to hurt, it can only do so if I allow it. If I react from impulse or reflex I am not free. I may, instead, take up the challenge and look at the issue from the offending person's point of view by asking whether perhaps what was said is correct. I want to know if there is a grain of truth in the statement. And if, with searching honesty, I can see some justification for it, I may be able to conclude that indeed what the other person said to me is largely justified and that now the situation suddenly appears in a new light. I now choose to see the other person not so much as an offender, whom I vehemently reject, but as someone who, possibly without meaning to, helped me understand myself better. Though the offence was probably intended, in the end it helped me go forward. Such thoughts filled with inner honesty will remove the emotional sting and replace it with inner calm because they help us focus on the integrity of the message and leave all else aside as unimportant. From such a fullness of soul we are shown concrete directions in which to proceed. Our moral imagination acquires wings for future actions.

We will not misunderstand the exercise as an attempt to confuse, to prove that green is red, for instance. We are not here to falsify reality by thinking improperly and less than truthfully. In the example cited the offence will always remain an offence, but we have gained another attitude towards it different from what we developed at the start. Inner tranquillity and thinking-awareness of the essentials prepare the way for moral intuitions and for the possibility that moral imagination becomes active in a creative way. We can thus see that, from our account of the exercise, a schooling of the feeling life appears beside that of thinking and willing.

Feelings normally come and go of themselves. Those who have strong and vibrant feelings know how overwhelmingly strong they can be and we are tempted to shrink from ever trying to control them, for fear of failure. But as we have just seen, feelings can be mastered by taking small and measured steps, one at a time. As long as feelings overwhelm us, we are their slave. They close off the path to freedom. Now it is not a matter of getting rid of feelings or of subduing them. But for those who want to be free the task is rather to gain a different relationship to them. We do not want to be their servant but to lead them and finally to mould them. This does not occur in the first encounter with our feelings but when we can survey them later during moments of self-chosen inner tranquillity. Striving for inner independence demands an awareness that certain outer circumstances set a train of feelings in motion, such as anger, irritation or despair. But now we look at them and ourselves from outside. Penetrating thoughts and creative ideas support the striving for self-control. They are the tools that transform and manage feelings. Since feelings are enkindled by mental images and ideas, new ideas are needed

to transform and control them. So long as we retain our old
ideas new feelings will arise only with difficulty. The key for
the transformation of feeling lies in thinking. Anger and
despair will always return as long as we hold fast to the idea,
for instance, that a certain person is out to make life difficult
for us. But once we have gained a new perspective through
clear thinking and we are convinced of its validity, the feelings will change. After a while we will find that the relationship between our ideas and feelings change in relation to
the circumstances we meet on the spot. We learn to guide our
thoughts and through them our feelings. In other words, our
judgements become less arbitrary, for they are now based
upon conscious and lucid thinking which in their turn give
direction to our feelings. We are thus on the path to freedom.
By means of the exercises here described, we learn to overcome more and more those barriers which, as part of our
make-up, stand in the way of *inner* freedom.

The next question is: 'How do we deal with the *outer*
factors that make us unfree?' The simple words of the
medieval philosopher Meister Eckhart may suggest a way
through the confusion of outer and inner limitations and
restrictions. He says: 'To stand aright within oneself means to
feel well amongst all people and in all places.' Nothing can
mitigate the truth of these words though we may not always
want to believe it. 'To stand aright within oneself means to
feel well amongst all people and in all places' says, in other
words, that it is always up to us to determine how we stand in
all the circumstances. Albrecht Haushofer for one did not
find his incarceration at all positive but he managed to draw
positive results from it. In the terror-filled darkness of his
situation he saw rays of light. It is not easy to see the light
when the soul feels itself in darkness, because it is initially
blind. But we can develop a new eye in the soul that can see
points of light in the darkness.

Rudolf Steiner has given us a fourth exercise which
enlarges the three we have just looked at. It shows us how to
open the inner eye of the soul so that we can see the hidden

light in darkness. Many circumstances in life give us the chance to seek a positive element among much that is negative. This does not mean that we ought to see life through rose-tinted glasses. It is rather an exercise in a genuine striving for knowledge. Haushofer did not at all gloss over the raw facts of his imprisonment. Black should not suddenly become white, but the white specks within the black can nonetheless be discovered.

It is easier again if we look back on past events. If, for example, at some time we have suffered an accident, we may have been initially overwhelmed by pain and taken it all as a tragic turn of destiny. But looking back now, it should be possible to see positive elements born out of the darkness of past suffering. Some people come to this without making an exercise of it. Life itself has led them to look at things in such a way. It may be difficult but not impossible to imagine that a man who lost a leg in the war might finally come to accept his lot with gratitude.

If we have managed to work through experiences of the past in the way described, it will become easier to work through present experiences and see them more clearly through the newly developed eye of the soul. Even for the most massive forms of unfreedom described earlier this will be valid, such as our powerlessness in contemporary life towards the destruction and pollution of nature. Once again it is not a matter of glossing over very real dangers or saying that things are not nearly as bad as they appear. We are not asked to see mitigating circumstances or to avoid facing the situation. Nevertheless, it is possible to think through the issues and find ways and means to live with them and work on. Everyone can develop creative ideas. It lies, for instance, in the realm of possibility that an ecological catastrophe will make future life on earth impossible. But it does not further my work to dwell on a thought of this kind, for it tends to hinder me rather than give me confidence. Therefore I take the thought seriously and don't avoid it, but I don't let it stop me from doing what is necessary.

During the present century we have already seen the collapse of several ideological systems. Fascism lasted for about one generation, a little shorter in Germany than in Spain. Then it collapsed, though of course its roots are still active in some minds. Communism in Europe, which collapsed a few years ago, lasted for two generations—a little longer in Russia, a little shorter in Eastern Europe. In the collapse of the Stalinist-Communist regime, many set their hopes on a new beginning, an alternative third way between liberal democratic capitalism and state-controlled party-capitalism. These hopes proved illusory in a relatively short time. The power of the Western economic system had been naively underestimated, beside the fact that no one was in the least prepared for the massive task ahead. But how long will the system of Western capitalism last which, in an embarrassingly presumptuous way, regards itself as the victor? How long will it too survive? If we begin our count from the epochal year 1917, is it going to last for three generations? This Western capitalist system has massive problems. It is not too far fetched, and may even be foresighted, to expect its collapse, but at the same time try to be more prepared for when this occurs. If we now want to conceive a better social model, we can begin by trying to formulate ideas that may take the place of the current ones. And this is the sign of the free spirit, as Rudolf Steiner describes it in *The Philosophy of Spiritual Activity*. He says: 'If the free spirit believes itself to have better ideas than those presently accepted, it seeks to put them into the place of the existing ones.'

In the Western world of today we may only be able to effect small changes, which is not a very uplifting perspective. Nor will a revolutionary spirit have an easy time accepting such a verdict. But taking a look back in history we can perceive how Lenin was a revolutionary who, with a very limited circle of like-minded people, prepared to change Russian society. He worked for many years without much hope of success. But his hour came and it found him well prepared. We may think of Lenin and his ideas how we will; that is not the point here, but we can certainly learn one thing from him. Through long years of despair he did not give up and his iron will enabled him to be ready when the tide of events changed in his favour. And if the time for our own ideas comes—if it ever does—at least we should not be unprepared. With this in mind, our work within its small confines and on its diminutive scale, will not seem like an exercise in futility.

Such or similar trains of thought are a beginning. They help us keep current issues in mind without resignation, and to seek for starting-points where we can take hold and put our own ideas into action. We are looking for positive signs which are able, in seemingly hopeless circumstances, to reveal a glimmer of hope. This exercise, done faithfully and systematically, directs our attention towards helpful and positive elements in current events. But its success depends largely on our ability to judge wisely.

We often ignore the fact that we are the ones who judge a given situation, and that our opinions, expectations and feelings are home-made. The free spirit wants to overcome this form of self-forgetfulness by *consciously* forming judgements and ideas, by which its feelings are enkindled. The apparent power of external circumstances need not be overwhelming if judgements are the result of careful and thorough thinking rather than of reflex-like prejudices.

Now certainly, only few people have enough inner strength to assess an unjust and life-threatening incarceration with an insight such as Albrecht Haushofer's. He overcame his initial reactions, regarded them as prejudices, and came to a new attitude towards his situation. He came to see his imprisonment in a different and deeply positive light. His feelings and emotions changed. In the place of fear and resentment he found confidence in the future and an inner calm. By doing so he identified himself with Meister Eckhart's words: 'To stand aright within oneself means to feel well amongst all people and in all places.' Haushofer, however, worked very hard to 'stand aright within [him]self'.

Anyone can begin such work towards becoming a free

spirit by taking on a fifth exercise which schools us gradually
to lay aside our prejudices. This takes time and can only be
done in small steps. We can begin by looking back at situations in which our judgements were inadequate or one-sided
and try to find out how they were formed. It is common
practice nowadays to make excuses for hasty judgements on
the grounds that the true facts were not known at the time.
For the purpose of the exercise such excuses are not valid.
Rather, they are obstacles in the way of self-knowledge. A
thorough and unsparing search for the source of prejudices
will uncover the reasons that tempted us to judge before we
knew all the relevant facts or why we failed to find them.
Having examined some of our prejudices in this way we will
be led to an extension of the exercise where we learn to judge
new situations more carefully and less impulsively. It is not an
easy task and we cannot expect to apply it all day because our
normal mechanism of judgement is too deeply ingrained in
us. But we can begin by consciously choosing a certain period
and occasion.

For example, if we know we are going to have a discussion
with friends, we can resolve to hold back our own judgement
during a certain part of the conversation. Normally we react
automatically to the statements of others with agreement or
disagreement. Even if we do not give voice to an opinion, our
thoughts and feelings form the judgements. But for the
duration of the exercise we refrain from forming any opinion
at all—we neither agree nor disagree. And yet we participate
actively in the conversation by listening carefully to the
words of the participants. At the beginning this is certainly
not easy and will not at once yield satisfying results. But if,
through force of habit, a judgement has crept in anyway, we
can help ourselves firstly by not voicing it and secondly by
gently asking or informing ourselves: '*How* did the other
person say what he did? *Why* would he feel like that?' Such
questions do not fully silence our own thinking, but they
soften our judgements and lead us away from too hasty 'right'
or 'wrong' assessments.

If on several occasions we have managed to still the urge to comment inwardly when listening to what others say, we can not only make the exercise longer but also act on the dismantling of our prejudices in new situations. Basically we are led to this by the exercise itself. Here too it is a matter of learning to suspend judgement.

In a conversation we may hear a remark that we know is quite incorrect. Say, for instance, that Goethe was born in 1748. At once our judgement intervenes: 'That is wrong. It was 1749, and there is no doubt about it.' But for the sake of the exercise we can disregard this certainty and leave open the possibility that new evidence might have been discovered to show that Goethe was born a year earlier than commonly thought. By doing such and similar exercises we gradually become less prone to prejudge. Further, we will be able in the long run to meet with open-mindedness unexpected events which we otherwise would not have thought possible. This fifth exercise can be added and practised in weekly or monthly rhythms in tandem with the four others.

The capacity to overcome the mechanisms of forming prejudgements is an important step on the path towards freeing oneself from the apparent constraint of outer restrictions. In this way we learn to react differently towards regulations and prohibitions. Even suffering under other people or under the conditions of time and space can be coped with in a new way. For to begin with, this suffering has mainly arisen as the result of our own prejudices. Even with sickness, death and blows of destiny we now win a new relationship. We can even make opinions on the past events of our life the object of the exercise, and by these means we can learn to face what comes with more equanimity. We will come to know how much in our experience of life depends on our own judgements and will therefore try to apply much greater care and circumspection—though no less energy—in coming to our conclusions.

Afterword

The foregoing discussions have tried to show that questions concerning the freedom of the human being cannot be answered in the form of general theoretical statements. Rather they have pointed to a realm of the soul where freedom can always freshly be achieved in practice if the individual wants it and sets out on the path towards it.

The aim of the text has been to facilitate the reader's understanding of the basic ideas in the second part of Rudolf Steiner's *Philosophy of Spiritual Activity*. It should not, however, be regarded as a substitute for reading the book itself. On the contrary, it is meant to encourage and prepare for the individual study of *The Philosophy of Spiritual Activity*. Nothing can take the place of Rudolf Steiner's book. It is rather the aim of this study to render itself superfluous in the long run, while the work it comments on should become more and more enlightening. If such should be the case, the author's intention will have been fulfilled.

Translator's Note

In a lecture on 14 March 1915 entitled 'The Secret of Death' Rudolf Steiner pointed out the impossibility of translating *Freiheit* by 'freedom', since the syllables *heit* and *tum* [dom] mediate quite different experiences. The first always leads into the realm of soul and spirit, suggesting mobility; the second leads more to external conditions. Thus, whenever the word 'freedom' appears it needs to be artistically recreated by the reader, otherwise it leads 'to errors of judgement which adversely affect life and cognition'. The book advances beyond mere freedom of choice to a pathway for becoming a free spirit, where the engagement of the human will is the advancing as well as the limiting agent. The title of the book *Der Wille Zur Freiheit* is thus translated: *The Will to be Free*.